Praise for *I Simply Have to Fall in Love*

Marina Tyurina has a philological background which enables her to embrace a wide spectrum of stylistic choices, from song lyrics to intellectual vers libre and per se prose.
—*Vyacheslav Kupriyanov, poet, Laureate of Ivan Bunin Prize*

Marina Tyurina Oberlander is a highly sophisticated poet. Her poetry findings are unpredicted and vibrant. The masterly "classic" verse blends with the philosophical vision of the world.
—*Victor Agranovich, composer*

Marina Oberlander's poetry is exceptionally visual. Her reality is transparent and precise. You feel an urge to put your hand on it.
—*Eugene Tsymbal, filmmaker*

Marina's poems are wonderful – in their manifold themes and techniques – they are sincere, but without anguish.
—*Alexander Smoljanski, filmmaker*

A true poet is said to be made of words and ruled by imagination. Marina belongs to this stock. Her individual voice is and always was rooted in her love of life.
—*Natalia Zhluktenko, PhD, Professor, Taras Shevchenko National University of Kyiv, Ukraine*

I SIMPLY HAVE
TO FALL IN LOVE

Marina Tyurina Oberlander

NAA NEW ACADEMIA PUBLISHING | SCARITH

Washington, DC

Library of Congress Control Number: 2020905481
ISBN 978-1-733398091 (alk. paper)

SCARITH   An imprint of New Academia Publishing

NEW ACADEMIA
PUBLISHING

New Academia Publishing
4401-A Connecticut Avenue NW #236, Washington DC 20008
info@newacademia.com - www.newacademia.com

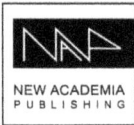

CONTENTS

PROLOGUE

I simply have to fall in love
with something or somebody
it may be cloud
it may be dove
a soul or a body
a twinkling star in stormy night
a tender voice from heaven
a touch of blessing in twilight
when poems pour in seven
a sheet of paper – blank and white
which I will stain with letters
or my next dream
which brings delight
and that is all that matters …

IN MEMORIAM

To Leonard

I'm still in love
up to the point
of your farewell – to disappoint
the life which was forever meant
to rise and burn until its end
the end came fast
and I'm alone
a *merry widow* on my own
with memories that live and last
and give temptation of the past
I feel your lips
I feel your hands
and your embrace that never ends …

MY TRIUMPH

I read my poems
standing straight
with nothing left to pay
I opened wide the iron gate
it was my triumph day

I felt your presence
you were there
not letting me to fall
of your support I was aware
and love was rising tall

I read my poems
and I knew
them you would always hear
and that my hand was reaching you
as if you were so near

whenever standing with my book
in front of crowd – I
will feel your hand
your gentle look
and love – until I die

You faded,
that one, with a scythe,
stood by, was ready for his entry.
Bare angel with a hearse, beside,
prepared for your departure gently.
Still clinging to your flesh and blood
so carelessly, in my affection,
I rushed myself into a rut
of earthly, soon, renunciation.
My hand fit your hand as a glove ...
I dreamt to get some magic powers –
disown the anguish, shield our love,
unbind the time from days and hours.
When, sadly bringing rest and peace,
God's mercy to our arms descended.
Eyes closed, two teardrops on your cheeks –
that's how the conversation ended.
As if you asked to be absolved
for giving not enough to treasure
and did forgive me for my love
which neither has an end nor measure.

Authorized translation by Igor Brailovski

You are the light
in sleepless night
a magic dream
a rapid stream
a waterfall
that takes it all
to soul's depth
of life and death
and struggles hard
through years apart
in wait
for our future date
when we unite
in heaven's flight

Today it was your day of birth
the casket lies in silent earth
which covered pain and disease
and feelings that are not for lease

but when I come and sit on grass
I sense your heart is beating fast
protecting me from evil mind
that wants to ruin from behind

and your everlasting smile
keeps me alive
at least a while

MEMORIAL DAY

On Memorial Day
memories pave the way
through the ocean wave
through the forest display
through the sunrise decay
through the sunset dismay
to the place where I stay
to the place where I pray
on a steep stairway
gone astray
to the margin of May
being touched by the ray
of memorial sway
today

ANNIVERSARY

Today like twenty years ago
I'll look at you –
hold out my hand
a silent touch
and you will know
it's time to put a wedding band
and thus unite us …

… you will go
I will remain
but the sand
of Chincoteague
that warmed our feet
will always warm my dreams
and fit
my memories
they are alive
like your spirit
in my life

IN THE EMBRACE
OF EROS

I fly towards flames
having spread my wings from the shoulders
and to what I do want
God himself won't give me an answer
dash around in yearning
for love
having cast all the doubts away
even acting against my conscience
crafty autumn is coming along
overwhelming with colors
striking me on the spot
and embracing with fair apparel
but my eyelashes
feel the cold
that is telling the fortune
of a snowfall
though the lock of embrace
burns with fire from nowhere expected
and the blade of a kiss
echoes back with a moan of passion
and with languor been drunk
flesh surrenders to your male strength

How long haven't I
been carried in someone's arms!

Translated by the Author

My God
that was a magic shock
when having touched your palms with mine
I felt the stream
from high above into the precipice of chime
and that's why entering the lift
lips in protracted kiss united
creating an alluring myth
of love – rejoicing and of missing
and later on
the song was sung
of bodies' power of alignment
impossibility of verge
to reach the limit of destruction

again circled in your arms
I swim in an inbidden capture
and feeling's fiery triptych
is drawing level of nirvana

Translated by the Author

Alas, poor Yorick!
Feel the chains
attaching me to sacred wall
of deep affection
which detains
my heart
my body
and my soul
I cannot fight
this love attraction
the misty feeling of delight
that brings award of satisfaction
into the morning
and the night
I tried to flee
but ties were massive
and pulled my mind close to thee
I only wish you do not mess me –
and make me what I want to be

I dreamt of sea
the sea was calm
we lay on grass
in shade of palm
and high above
the naughty breeze
played funny game
with mighty leaves
we lay embraced
your sunburnt chest
was pressed against
my naked breast
and passion poured
from searching lips
onto my lusting
body tips
I heard my own
ecstatic moan
that woke me up
I was alone
in my king size
half-empty bed
with tears in eyes
and soaking wet …

Life made a twist
and you exist
how sweet a feel
that you are real
my body glows
when you expose
yourself to me
erotic melodie
streams through the space
of our embrace
and I surrender to your might
in awesome flight …

You wanted snow
here it came
but there is no fireplace
to sit in front in soft embrace
and look at tongues of dancing flame
with hand in hand in sweet caress
to take a sip of sparkling wine
and pray to God for tender bless
of lasting love and the good time …

The snow is gone
the rain washed
leftovers from the grass
I was at home
and on my own
watching the day to pass

This day is gone
it was not bad
it left my woes behind
of me alone
being sad
and opened up my mind
for sun to come
and warm my hand
so it could write a verse
by putting pressure with my thumb
on pen which is my curse ...

I've never been as lonely as today
maybe it was just certain Saturday
when kids went out to the streets to play
and streets appeared to be bright and gay
I walked along a narrow hide-a-way
the falling leaves were covering my way
I stepped on them as on the golden tray
and felt the smell of their fall decay
the scent of love was filling broadway
and I was happy in a certain way
what can I say about this betray
my cherished wish is that you come
and stay ...

I am tired of loving myself
in the darkness of night
fantasizing about your touches
like a little and lonely elf
I am waiting for light
that is promising, sultry and luscious
I am waiting for glamorous day
when you come not to leave
but remain with me for a while
when you find a reason to stay
and to make me believe
in your open dependable smile
for I felt like your half
in your arms being flown
and aroused by lusting incitement

I am tired of loving myself
and of dancing alone
just recalling the dream of excitement

I miss you so much, my dear
my lust is getting high
I want you close
I want you near
and that I can't deny
I think of you when I am awake
and on my way to bed
when drinking wine or eating steak
when being glad or sad
I dream of you
I long for you
for your tight embrace
my fragile hope
like morning dew
will wet your sleepy face
and in the middle of the night
you'll hear my silent sigh
the wrap of words I only write
to love that won't die ...

Speak softly love
that leads to passion
and lasts until the very peak
of pleasure
feeling kisses deep
and bodies' powerful compression

I live through an eternal lust
for your embrace
and tender touches
speak softly love
it is a must
that never measures by its muchness

Where do I start
for distant run
I'm young at heart
and life is fun
with sing and dance
with smile and laugh
and open chance
that's not enough

What do I wait
for blooming rose
or for a bait
to be exposed
to someone hot
with gentle hands
who talks a lot
and understands

The life is short
get what you wish
and be a sport
to break and dish

You tamed me
I miss you in the night
when stars are bright
when everything is quiet
and I just write
you aimed at me

I feel your arms
embracing me in bed
I feel your body
pressed against mine
and whisper softly
going through my head
of your words
that build a caring shrine

Let time pass
and worries go away
don't be afraid
that I will ever leave you
love is a gift
and not a game to play
your only way
is to believe me …

I haven't talked to you tonight
and I feel incomplete
the Moon is gone
the stars are bright
and make the bedroom lit
I missed your call
I was away
I haven't heard the ring
and dreamt of all
what you could say
but time cut the link …

I'm used to hear
your soothing voice
before I go to sleep
and grab, my dear
the given choice
of feeling kisses deep
wherever path
of sudden match
will take – we can't predict
we do not need to start from scratch
but this may be a pick …

It was raining today
from the morning till night
there was awkward delay
of the sunshine bright
it's predicted to come
in a day or in two
my inadvertent calm
what to do
should I do?
I am yearning for you
should I trust?
should I wait?
like a soul in a queue
I have swallowed the bait
I have taken the chance
I am falling in love
and I thirst for romance
with the stars high above

Today was a gloomy and rainy day
it took you from me and it took you away
and all the tears that I could have shed
fell on the overcrowded parkway bed
where my car sailed as a perfect boat …

Now I bear an unbearable load
of lust that I cannot forever expose
to anyone else but a yellow rose

I cannot tell you what you miss
you won't believe what I am missing
I miss the taste
of your kiss
and your embrace that makes me blissing
your fiery whisper in my ear
and final delicate intrusion
into my bosom
when the gear
appears to be a sheer illusion
I miss the reach of pleasure peak
when heart is pounding and beating
and your satisfying shriek
the act of love with me completing

how long I longed for being kissed
the depth of night was only wissing
I couldn't tell you what I missed
you wouldn't believe what you were missing
and maybe in a bunch of years
my glance will strike you to the bottom
and your eyes will fill with tears
because love was not forgotten …

I still don't believe
that what happened to us wasn't real
that the day
which emerged with a passion
left nothing to feel
but melancholy
pouring with rain from the cloudy skies
and awaiting for Sun
warming up inaffectionate eyes
I still don't believe
that your message will never arrive
that your kiss was a fake
and your look was a blade of a knife
that a moment of love
being born
won't expand
won't last
and will slowly fade
in the mist of a wonderful past

The scar within my soul you left
is fresh
the sorrow filled the bowl
of passion
which was just a theft
from life
where I did not belong
like cup of Taiwan tea Oolong
cannot be drunk by coffee mate
but I recall our rainy date
and your umbrella like a pledge
sits on the fragile basket edge ...

It was a story of lust – the last
it was a story of past – that passed
of love that failed to emerge
and ended up in hopeless search
of breaking up my solitude
of my enjoyment lying nude
with you in bed once lonsome cold
for so long ...
Payoff was bold.

FAREWELL

What can I say – if nothing in return
what can I feel – if nothing in compassion
the life is real but it has made a turn
and nothing seems as awkward as obsession

I was awake and opening my soul
to your embrace and space of hot desire
I drank my lust from everlasting bowl
and our heads and bodies were on fire

The fire died and no sparkle left
the once big ardor turning into ashes
you can't enjoy the happiness of theft
and drops that fall from overcoming splashes

Farewell to love my soul has not met
and wasn't given adequate reception
I am no slave of unfulfilled intent
I won't pray for idols of deception

The lust was strong
I waited long
your promise lived
like hidden treasure
to give no less
than sweet caress
and deepest kiss without measure

but binding thread
which made us mad
became weak
just in a moment
and did not hold
the feeling bold
its breaking ending in a torment

my loving soul
expressed it all
with sharpened words
on piece of paper
the lust is gone
I am alone
and you are no one I would care

Say what is love
it's God and Devil
embracing us from very start
pull up and down
like good and evil
and coexist in every heart

your spirit glares in abstraction
creating dreams in endless turn
but sweet desire of seduction
turns body into fire burn

and body melts
with falling crown
and it surrenders to the might
of other body
which surrounds
with overpower of light

that takes you up
and brings you down
and tears your fragile soul apart
but morning meets
its misty dawn
and new beginning fills my heart

24 HOURS

Evening

caress
charm
kiss

Night

embrace
posession
solitude

Morning

dreams
melancholy
hunger

Day

breakfast
exertion
oblivion

Translated by the Author

Today it rains
again
I search for sun in vain
should I complain?
Impossible
the rain won't stop
even if you pray
is it his gain?

He mocks me
his power is strong
he welcomes me
to walking in his might
to make me wet
and thus forget
the sorrows
he is right
he washes off
the layers of regret
that I have met
and what's ahead?
The Light

From the book
ON THE SHARP EDGE
OF SPACE

Original title,
Na ostrom rubezhe prostranstva, 2008

BALLAD OF HAPPINESS

Destinies crossing…
Boris Pasternak

The Moon was shining in the sky
looking in the window
and something was crying in me
and something was singing

no
we did not need words
and we were silent
and floated into the sea of dreams
away from all sorrows

as soon as blackness of the night
fell upon us
my dream merged with your dream
in its obscurity

and at this hour
blessed by God
the years that have been lived before
and all the troubles vanished

gulping down the stars
we eagerly drank
transparent air of the night
saturated with dew

the Moon was shining in the sky
looking at us
and something was crying in me
and something singing

Translated by the Author

I wish it rains
I can't breathe
my solitude
is prison of my soul
you wait
what do you wait
my Mother Nature for
you wait for rain
it will fix the things
I wait for it as well
it is a remedy for thoughts
they press my mind
if there's a lot of them
but rain comes
and soothes everything
anxiety will dull
and gentle tap
of timid drops
is balm

I love you so
when you come
and at this time
I like to long
for something
that wasn't realized
forgive me
who am I asking for forgivness?
the rain

It happened once to me
there was no rain
but simply
the organ played
its music poured
like streams
on cold and naked roof
and I forgot my pain
like in rain
I was deceived
but I forgave
who? – yes, the organ
cause it's dependent
on fingers
and rain is free

The sound of drops
is getting softer
and happiness is filling
my heart
the rain stopped
don't cry …

Translated by the Author

FEARS

Fear
before meeting
fear
before parting
fear
before a crowd
fear
of solitude
fear
before despair
fear
before love
fear
before the door
fear
of separation
fear
of the unknown
fear
before life
fear
before God
fear
of death

Translated by the Author

A year of love
a year
relative
to a term of life

a year of love
a moment
relative
to eternity

a year of love
eternity
relative
to a moment

a year of love
a year
a moment
eternity

Translated by the Author

MASKS

Awakening in the morning
I take off the mask
of weariness
putting on the mask
of joy
to meet the coming day

at noon
taking off the mask
of joy
putting on the mask
of concern

taking it off
at lunch
putting on a mask
of placidity

in the evening
switching to the mask
of mysteriousness

before going to sleep
tête-à-tête with myself
I try
all masks
finding
which suits me best
and put on
the mask of weariness
to take it off
in the morning

Translated by the Author

First Morning
when nobody came to help
first time
when there was no one
to ask for advice
as if on purpose
when I needed it most
everybody was gone
left me alone
the space surrounding me
so familiar
suddenly became strange
and obscure
everyone turned away
giving me the right
to leave childhood on my own
the day
when my baby cup
fell and broke
slipping through mother's hands

Translated by the Author

My unrequited love
only mine
nobody
knows about it
maybe it's for the best
that it is not returned by you
it is only inside me
nobody will notice it
won't laugh at it
won't be jealous of it
my unrequited love
only my
love

Translated by the Author

Telephone does not ring
it fell silent
as if its sound melted
as if its voice vanished
and the world got empty
the world got deaf
withdrew into itself
the lamps are tired to wait
the mirror is tired to call
the clock is tired to go
it waits
but the phone does not ring
it is glued to the wall
it hid itself in the wall
turned its back
why is it silent
why did it get numb
as if it was replaced
by emptiness
I know
there is a reason
I should not wait any more
but I do

Translated by the Author

A DATE WITH APRIL

Railway station
train
car
I am going on a date with April
in September
as if everything
can be turned around
September turned
into April
yellow leaves turned
into unopened buds
the scent of autumn
ousted by the smell of yet unmelted snow
as if
time cities feelings
can be mixed
as if
the trembling of the frozen fingers
can be soothed
as if
the starting train
can be stopped
relentless train
taking April from me
leaving me
yellow leaves
lavishly thrown under my feet
by the wind
yellow leaves
the symbol of parting
merciless train
leaving me
in September

Translated by the Author

I write
in volleys
sighs
revelations
every word of mine
is a revelation
before myself
before people
before God
every word of mine
is a sigh
that it is in the past
a sigh
having let this word
out into life
a sigh
that I will never
write
likewise

Translated by the Author

FATHER'S PHOTO

Looking at me
from behind the glass doors
of the book-case
smiling
your unseen for anyone
but me
smile
if the door opens
what? ...
a willow is weeping
at the Novodevichy*
leaning over
the black memorial

Translated by the Author

---

* *Novodevichy Cemetery is a historic cemetery in Moscow, Russia.*

TRINITY

Poetry is music of words
music is poetry of sounds
set one to the other
and a song will emerge
there is nothing but a voice
to be found to sing it

Past
does not return
even
if you meet it
face to face
turn your back
because
it has to remain behind

Going to meet
a new day
glance back
with tears in your eyes

Translated by the Author

Rain
rain
rain all day
rain all night
raindrops tap on the windows
try to get into the room
find a dry spot
to fall on it
look for coziness

grey clouds
wonder in the sky
in search of the Sun
sky in despair
yearns for blue color
white clouds
the rainbow
yearns for smiles
smiles of the Sun in the pools
childrens' laugh
lovers' kisses

raindrops
tears of the sky
knock on the windows
creep into the room
touch my shoulders
embrace me with cold and sadness
fill my heart
with desire of sunshine

rain
rain in the street
rain in the whole world
rain in my heart

Translated by the Author

THROES OF CREATION

Run to the desk
with thoughts in your head

and stiffen with a pencil
in search of words

If you have to buy
love
with betraying
your own ideas
is it worth
such a sacrifice?

Emerald
a green eye
of my soul
a green flower
of my love
the green teardrop
on my hand

Translated by the Author

A mosquito whines
over my head
promising another sleepless night
which started in the morning

Someone else's windows
someone else's world
do not peep in them
think if you'd want anybody
to peep in your heart

Spring breaks off into the summer
summer flies away into autumn
autumn falls off into winter
winter sinks into spring

Authorized translation by Renata Moldavskaya

From the book
MUSIC OF WORDS

(Original title, *Muzyka slov*, 2013)

AGILE

Sunset is flashing through the branches.
They've shed their leaves.
Rotunda's columns are white sentries.
They're guarding peace.
The sky's blue shawl turns dark. It's showing
embroidered stars.
A whisper of a kiss is floating.
Embarrassed sighs
are gliding shyly through the veiling
of fading light.
Two happy silhouettes are melting
into the night.

Authorized translation by Igor Brailovski

I won't understand the disbelief
and those orators
twined with heartlessness
who try to erase the Holocaust
from memory
as a letter from the alphabet

the tragedies
apparently
are not respected
by some favorites of fortune
who strive to distract awareness
as of evil days
where torn strings
sound more and more muted

birds over stubble
remnants of a slashed trail
here THEY were buried under soil
and even were grudged on bullets
nobody sang the International
but quietly and submissively prayed
and the loose hill did not cry for revenge
but simply stirred for three days

eagerly the town preferred to forget
that it was depopulated by one third in one day
that the calamity has taken place
and that the Jews are primordially humans

let some assume the Holocaust a myth
I do not need other evidence
but that grave overgrown with grass
where people were buried alive

Translated by the Author

FOUR EVENINGS
(a joke)

> By the window I sit. I have washed the dishes.
> I was happy here. I won't be any more.
>
> *Joseph Brodsky*

I read a novel. And in that novel
Margarita destroys my Arbat home.
Satan accompanies Christ to heaven,
and the saucy Cat tries to get on a street-car.
    I sit at the table. There is wine on the table.
    Bread. Roquefort. Tomato. It is dark outside.

I read poetry. And in the poems
Leaves fall into dust on the margins of the page.
Puffy clouds drift in the skies
And hurriedly call me to join them.
    I sit at the table. There is cognac on the table.
    Chocolate. Grapes. There is night behind the window.

I went to the shop and bought some food.
Cooked dinner. Brought water from the well.
It occurred to me: the borscht's horror is in the pot,
the burger's – in the pan, and the gristle's – in the aspic.
    I sit at the table. There is caviar on the table.
    It means that it's time to fill my glass with vodka.

I washed the dishes. Laundered the clothes.
Fixed the vacuum cleaner and tidied up my home.
Cut down a dead tree and feed the fire in the fireplace.
I loved you. I don't love you any more.
    I sit at the table. Drink "Veuve Cliquot".
    There is darkness outside. And a lightness in my heart.

Translated by the Author

PAINTING
(I DO NOT CARE 57)

To Victor Freso

A green background
squares and veils
a crafty web of strokes and lines
and vivid rise of a spinning spiral
not projecting deceleration of the flight

I look into the vortex
and feel – I penetrate
into the square of a soul
with a canvas outline
but hear the sigh:
I DO NOT CARE
and contemplate
which time is this?
Yeah… the fifty-seventh

Translated by the Author

FOUNTAIN HOUSE

It was very scary to live in that house
Anna Akhmatova

The Fountain House ghosts don't rest, in pain,
they live inside the "Poem Without Hero".
The grim facade is washed by streams of rain,
the fog is crawling over cloudy river.
Where Anna's spirit – trampled by the time
of deaf and mute – still outlived her era.

That house had become a scary nest
when, pillaged by newcomers – horde of golems –
it still exuded memories of the past
as if it were enchanted by her poems,
despite the crumbling colored stained glass
and binding chains of gloom around its columns.

Her heroes' woeful score would try and try
escaping from the dungeon's rugged walls.
To fall into despair and simply die
was unbecoming. Then, inside her soul,
awakened a true mother who would fight,
would not sell out to the rule for gold.

They took away her son to make her tame,
renounce poems, essence, thoughts and dreams,
get used to the captivity, restraints,
respectably pour dregs to the mainstream.
She covered then her candle, saved the flame
from the relentless biased judges' screams.

The Fountain House never left behind
the memory of her; it kept connection.
Lost phantom of the past – a precious find –

is still alive in distant recollections …
A wreath of love, so magically entwined
with her unhappened dates, break-ups, confessions.

Authorized translation by Igor Brailovski

IN MEMORY OF OSIP MANDELSTAM

… Executions – are major obsession
Of this bloody broad-chested Ossetian.
Osip Mandelstam

The night came down
the rumble of the wheels
ripped souls apart without a slight compassion
you knew the gloom of your tomorrow's chills
rejecting even slim misapprehension

the past was left behind and faded fast
Voronezh*
Nadya
summertime
a flower
behind a stone wall
in dingy reign of Death
Grim Reaper ruled with reckless savage power

then on the way
the grief and sorrow fled
and body froze its each and every member
Vladivostok loomed viciously ahead –
the prison cell
the 'can'
the torture chamber

but Poet in your torn and tired soul
did not allow you to become a bondsman
and you returned so proudly after all
and cleared your candid poetry and name

your poems were so heartfelt
sharp and true
despite the Fate's hard blows and painful tosses
that even *'Bloody Butcher'* thanks to you
is doomed to live forever in your verses

Authorized translation by Renata Moldavskaya

—

Voronezh – city in southwestern Russia, where O. Mandelstam lived in exile in 1935-38 with his wife Nadezhda (Nadya) between his first (1934) and second arrest (1938).
'Bloody Butcher' – Joseph Stalin.

From the Art Catalogue
RUSSIA – PARALLEL REALITY

(in English and Russian, Moscow, 2016)
Authorized translation by Galina Rud'

LANDSCAPE FROM MEMORY

To Vladimir Khamkov

There is a live canvas
on a yellow wall,
a carmine house with
heaven aflame. All

green windows gleaming
against sunlight.
The cloud's cocoon swimming,
embraced by green sight.

By rote the painter
displayed his paysage
with shadowy air,
the sparse entourage.

But who's near the house?
The contour is wrong,
the wide open mouth
refers to a song.

The space sighing out,
the colours are thick,
the freedom is blowing,
forgotten, from scene.

At night I will dream it:
a world with no sides.
In sky is a blue tit,
Hamkov is inside.

NORILSK

To Alexander Strakh

Stuck in the air –
black chimneys' ghosts.
Who would take care
of burning frost?
There is blue heaven
in rusty scab.
The priest is praying
on the church step.

Tundra's burnt out,
no moss, nor reeds.
Platinum ground –
pure benefits.
Cobalt,
palladium,
nickel and brass,
someone would have them
easily, thus,
stronghold of power
is Divine faith.
The brimstone cloud
floats to the place.
There's panorama –
Pipes and snow fuse …
Camera's my karma,
it shows the truth.

SELFIE

Dear sir, what is your parallel? Please, answer,
what's your reality right now? Is it luck?
You know, honestly, I doubted, oh brother,
when spotted you amidst the city park.

With truly loving eyes you led a maiden,
as brave boyfriend, a gallant cavalier,
then clicked the selfie while embracing hangmen,
against dead letters, which are C-C-C-P.

PHOTO LINE

There is drifting snow,
the blizzard has calmed,
hiding a boy's nose
inside a long scarf.

From beneath the hat his eyes
look at me so fine,
as if welcoming a nice,
brand new photo line.

I'll take snaps of boundless
icy foam-white space,
chains of distant mountains
and an old sleigh race,

a white doggy's muzzle
of a sage – a watch.
Abstract view is, rather,
a cat on the porch.

MOMENT

I seized the moment –
the hair is blown above.
In smiling eyes astonishment is gracing,
that there's a clear equivalent of love,
the worth of which is the Almighty blessing.

TAYMYR

Atlantic is a cradle of cyclones.
Taymyr is called the graveyard of whirlwinds.
We don't hear the twitter of birdsongs,
and life is lived by nature's own orders,

dictated by the rigour of the cold,
by permafrost, lay underfoot, the blinding
white purity of virgin land, so old,
and caustic gales, which blow strong and winding.

But matchless northern flowers – bright-hot –
bloom in the summer, rising from the ice hell.
The town was erected in spite of
north whimsicality and local way of life. Well,

I look at snaps made by your skillful hand
with a long line of open countenances
and see the rising star above the land
of loving persons, sorrows, dreams and fancies ...

CHIMNEYS

Whether twilight or early dawn –
city mires in hazy shade.
Chimneys labor mightily long
generating hell on the land.

They are hard to condemn for that.
Their creator, dispersed in shade,
laid to rest Ariadne's thread
in the want of his own land.

From the heavenly cloudy road
you see chimneys' dance in the shade,
spasms of beauty squeezing your throat –
unexplainable on the land.

AUTHENTICITY

Snow is falling on Moscow's small alleys.
Reindeer herd. A plaster Putin.
Bridge over Neva is raised above blackness.
Felix's suspended. Iron bars suiting.
The Kremlin Cup. A girl with a ball.
Putin in field cap. Vive, Russia! Deity.
Skolkovo. Ladder. Soil. The hole.
Crows in the sky. House is rickety.

What am I – in the dimension I live?
Sense of existence is grasped, clearing muddle
by steeple of church on the float with a reeve
or my reflection, perhaps, in a puddle …

EPILOGUE

I PLAY THE MELODY OF LOVE
that keeps my soul high above
the prose of life
and life's routine
and makes me fly
into a dream
the dream where wishes stay alive
and lust is waiting for delight
of tasty kiss
and tender touch

Is this a wish I dream too much
is this a dream I wish to clutch
and on the keys that I will play
you'll see the image I display ...

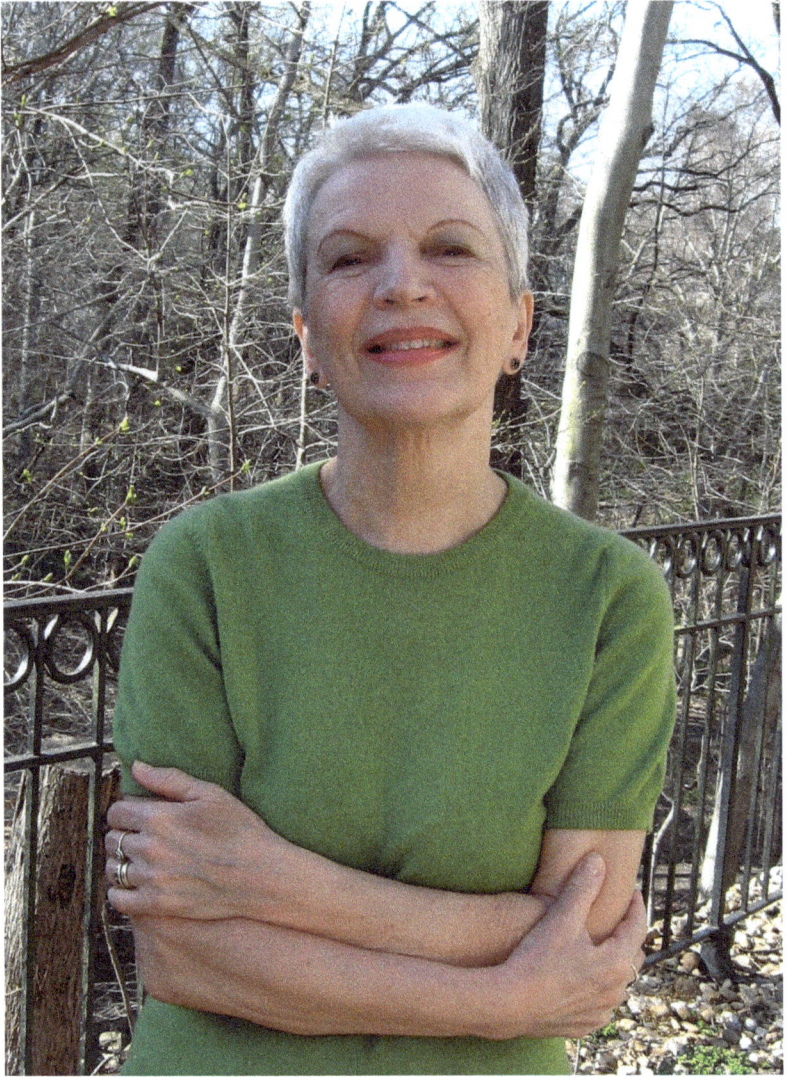

ABOUT THE AUTHOR

Marina Tyurina Oberlander is a poet, writer and well-known translator of Scandinavian and English prose and poetry into Russian, member of the Writers' Union of the XXI Century and Laureate of the International Leonardo da Vinci Prize (2018).

Among her translations are poetry books of the Nobel Prize nominee Inger Christensen and a prominent contemporary Danish poet Søren Ulrik Thomsen, as well as the book *Denmark and Russia – 500 Years*, a history of diplomatic relations between the two countries.

She is author of three books, all published in Moscow: *Na ostrom rubezhe prostranstva* (*On the Sharp Edge of Space*, 2008), which comprises her own poems and translations into Russian of Danish, Norwegian and American poetry; *Muzika Slov* (*Music of Words*, 2013), a collection of more than 200 poems and six short stories; and *Vysokaya Nota* (*High Note*, 2020), a collection of about 150 poems, five stories and three essays; and numerous publications in prestigious literary journals in Russia, USA, Germany and Iran.

A CD with 12 songs composed by Victor Agranovich on Marina's poetry, *Kogda vryvaetsya lyubov'* (*When Love Barges in*) was released in 2014.

Marina Tyurina Oberlander was born in St. Petersburg (Leningrad), Russia, into the family of a world renowned soil scientist, Ivan V. Tyurin. She holds a Master's Degree in Philology from Moscow State University. After completing post-graduate studies at the same university, she taught Danish at the Diplomatic Academy and, for more than a decade, worked

84

as an editor at two of the largest publishing houses in Russia – Progress and Raduga.

Since 2000, Marina Tyurina Oberlander has lived in Washington, D.C. This book of poetry is her first publication in English.

ABOUT THE ARTIST

The book is illustrated by Marina's grandson, Konstantin Ferdinand Weber-Chubays, a young prodigy, who illustrated both her translated books of Inger Christensen's and Søren Ulrik Thomsen's poetry, and her own third book of poetry and prose.